MANIPULATION AND DARK PSYCHOLOGY

Learn to Read People Quickly, Discover
Deceptions, Defend Yourself from Toxic People,
Recognizing the Techniques of Persuasion and
Emotional Manipulation

By

Robert Meyer

Disclaimer Notice:

Please note the information contained within this document is for educational and entertainment purposes only. All effort has been executed to present accurate, up to date, and reliable, complete information. No warranties of any kind are declared or implied.

Readers acknowledge that the author is not engaging in the rendering of legal, financial, medical, or professional advice. The content within this book has been derived from various sources. Please consult a licensed professional before attempting any techniques outlined in this book.

Table of Contents

INTRODUCTION

The aim of emotional manipulation is to influence the behavior of another person by means of certain tactics that may or may not be clear to the person being manipulated or anyone else. The aim may not only be to change the behavior of the manipulated, but also to convince him that there is no alternatives and that his relationship with the manipulator is inevitable. Although it may not be as obvious as other forms of abuse, it is still considered as abuse. Emotional manipulation is considered as emotional abuse that may or may not be associated with other forms of abuse, such as physical and sexual abuse.

There is a difference between persuasion and emotional manipulation. Persuasion is not coercive and respects the right of the person to choose and to accept or reject the behavior suggested. In the case of manipulation, it may seem superficial that the person is allowed to choose. However, under the superficial pretense of freedom of choice, there is an undercurrent of emotional coercion.

The manipulators are on a spectrum of different characters. However, they are all characterized by personality abnormality. It is easy to identify a merciless, cruel, callous, and remorseless psychopath. However, some other disordered individuals may use manipulation to survive their own pathology and maintain their psychological integrity. An emotionally dependent person may seek his emotional needs by manipulating others. The same for those with narcissistic personality where someone tries to fulfill their desire for power, prestige, vanity and self-aggrandization by manipulating others. Histrionics seeking attention, self-indulgence, and satisfaction of superficial emotional and sexual needs may use all their seductive and dramatic exaggerations to manipulate others. People with borderline personality disorder, with their chaotic emotions and sense of inner emptiness, dramatic mood swings, impenetrable adventures and acting out, will manipulate others just by their aggression or self-harm.

The manipulator is trying to control the manipulated to maintain his emotional or personal gains. Some manipulators can easily shift their focus from one victim to another, but others can end up struggling to keep their victim under their claws. The most vulnerable to manipulation are those peaceful and timid people who lack self-confidence. They're usually conscientious, submissive, honest, and often naive. They may be lonely, traumatized, and seek refuge in the hands of a powerful manipulator. In fact, they may even lack self-respect, with a deep sense of guilt that seeks punishment, and a feeling that they deserve to be punished. Even those who have the ability to intellectualize about their life dilemmas can deceive themselves by working hard on the hidden, understandable reasons for the manipulator's actions. They find excuses for the perpetrator, but ignore the obvious need to free themselves from the hands of the manipulator. They enjoy intellectualizing about their suffering as they find their vulnerability too painful to live with.

You will discover the tips, secrets and techniques of manipulation and dark psychology in this book. The book will help you learn about the use of dark psychology that will help prevent you from being manipulated. Additionally, you will also understand the tricks of seduction and find out how to treat a toxic person.

CHAPTER ONE

DARK PSYCHOLOGY

Dark Psychology is an art and science of mind control and manipulation. While Psychology is a study of human behavior and is central to our thoughts, actions, and interactions, the term Dark Psychology is a phenomenon that describes how people use motivation, persuasion, manipulation, and coercion tactics to get what they want.

All of humanity has the potential to victimize other human beings and living creatures. While many are restraining or sublimating this tendency, some act upon these impulses. Dark Psychology seeks to understand the thoughts, feelings and perceptions that lead to human predatory behavior. Dark Psychology assumes that this production is objective and has some rational, goal-oriented motivation 99.99 percent of the time. The remaining 0.01 percent, under Dark Psychology, is the brutal victimization of others without intention or a reasonable definition under evolutionary science or religious dogma.

The more you can see Dark Psychology, the better prepared you will be to reduce your chances of victimization by human predators. It is important to have a minimal understanding of Dark Psychology before proceeding. As you move through future manuscripts to expand this construction, this writer will go into the details of the most important concepts. The following six tenets are needed to fully understand Dark Psychology:

1. Dark Psychology is a general part of the human state. This construction has had an influence throughout history. All cultures, societies and people who reside in them maintain this aspect of the human condition. The most benevolent people are known to have this realm of evil but never act upon it and have lower rates of violent thoughts and feelings.

2. Dark Psychology is simply the study of the human condition as it relates to people's thoughts, feelings, and perceptions of this innate potential to prey upon others without clear, definable reasons. Given that all behavior is purposeful, goal-oriented, and conceptualized through modus operandi, Dark Psychology puts forward the notion that the closer a person gets to the "black hole" of pristine evil, the less likely he has a motivational purpose. Although this writer assumes that pristine evil is never attained since it is infinite, Dark Psychology assumes that there are some who come close.

3. Dark Psychology can be overlooked in its latent form because of its potential for misinterpretation as aberrant psychology. History is full of examples of this latent tendency to reveal itself as active and destructive behavior. Modern psychiatry and psychology define the psychopath as a predator who has no remorse for his actions. Dark Psychology maintains that there is a continuum of severity ranging

from feelings and thoughts of violence to serious victimization and violence without a significant purpose or motivation.

4. On this continuum, the seriousness of the Dark Psychology is not considered to be less or more abominable by the behavior of victimization, but it plots a range of inhumanity. A simple illustration would be a comparison between Ted Bundy and Jeffrey Dahmer. They were both severe psychopaths and heinous in their actions. The difference is that Dahmer committed his atrocious murders on account of his illusory need for companionship while Ted Bundy sadistically inflicted pain on others as a result of sheer psychiatric evil. Both would be higher in the Dark Continuum, but Jeffrey Dahmer can be better understood for his psychotic desperate need to be loved.

5. Dark Psychology assumes that all people have a zeal for violence. This zeal is innate in all humans, and various external and internal factors can increase the likelihood of this potential manifesting itself in volatile behaviors. These behaviors are predatory in nature and can sometimes function without reason. Dark Psychology assumes that the predator-prey dynamic is distorted by humans. Dark Psychology is merely a human phenomenon and is not shared by any other living creature. Violence and chaos may exist in other living organisms, but humanity is the only species that has the potential to do so without purpose.

6. Understanding the underlying causes of Dark Psychology would make it easier for society to recognize, diagnose and possibly reduce the hazards inherent in its influence. Learning the concepts of Dark Psychology has a twofold beneficial effect. First, by accepting that all of us have this potential for evil, it allows those with this knowledge to reduce the likelihood that it will erupt. Second, grasping the tenets of Dark Psychology fits our original evolutionary goal of struggling to survive.

Dark Psychology Triads

Narcissism – Egotism, grandiosity, and lack of sympathy.

Machiavellianism – Uses manipulation to mislead and exploit people with no sense of morality.

Psychopathy – Often charming and friendly, yet characterized by impulsiveness, selfishness, and lack of sympathy and remorse.

None of us need to be a victim of manipulation, but that happens quite often. We may not be subject to people specifically in the Dark Triad, but normal, everyday people like you and I may face dark psychology tactics.

These tactics are often found in internet advertisments, commercials, sales techniques, and even in the behavior of our manager at work. If you have kids, you will likely experience these tactics as your kids experiment with behaviors to get what they need and seek autonomy. In fact, dark persuasion and covert manipulation are often used by people whom you trust and love. Here are some of the tactics most commonly used by ordinary, everyday people.

Love Flooding – Using Affection, compliments, or buttering someone up

Lying – Using exaggeration, falsehood, partial truths, untrue stories

Love Denial – Withholding attention and affection

Withdrawal – Avoiding human or silent treatment

Choice Restriction – Give certain choices that distract you from the choice that you do not want someone to create.

Reverse Psychology – Tell someone one thing or do something to motivate them to do the opposite, which is what you really want

Semantic Manipulation – Using words that have a mutual definition, after which the manipulator will tell you that he or she has a different definition and understanding of the conversation. Words are powerful, and they import.

This serves to remind us all how easy it is to use these tactics to get what we want. I want to motivate you to check your tactics in all areas of life, including work, leadership, parenting, romantic relationships, and friendships.

While some individuals who use these dark tactics know what they're doing, and they're willing to manipulate you to get what they want, others use dark and unethical tactics without being fully aware of it. Many of these people learned the tactics of their parents during childhood. Others have learned tactics in their teenage years or adulthood by accident. They used manipulation tactics inadvertently, and it worked. They've got what they wanted. They, therefore, continue to use tactics that will help them to get their way.

In some cases, people learn how to use such tactics. Training procedures that teach dark, psychological and persuasion tactics are usually sales or marketing programs. Many of these processes use dark tactics to create a brand or to sell a product for the sole purpose of serving themselves or their company, and not the client. Many of these training programs influence people to believe that using such tactics is all right and to the benefit of the buyer because their lives will be much better when they buy a product or service.

Who is using Dark Psychology and Manipulative Tactics? Here is a list of people who use these tactics most often.

Narcissists – People who are truly narcissistic have inflated self-esteem. They need others to validate their belief that they are superior. They have dreams of being worshiped. They use the tactics of dark psychology, manipulation, and unethical persuasion to maintain this.

Sociopaths – People who are really sociopathic (meeting clinical diagnosis) are often charming and intelligent, yet impulsive. Due to a lack of emotion and remorse, they use dark tactics to build a superficial relationship and then take advantage of people.

Attorneys – Some lawyers are so intent on winning their case that they use dark persuasion tactics to get the outcome they want.

Politics – Some politicians use dark psychological tactics and dark persuasion tactics to convince people that they are right and to get votes.

Sales People – Many salespeople are so focused on selling that they use dark tactics to motivate and convince someone to purchase their product.

Leaders – Some leaders acquire dark tactics to obtain compliance, greater effort, or higher work ethics from their subordinates.

Public Speakers – Some speakers acquire and use dark tactics to heighten the emotional state of the audience, knowing that it leads to more products being sold in the back of the room.

Selfish People – This can be anyone who puts themselves in front of others. They will use tactics to meet their own needs, even at the expense of someone else. They do not mind the win-loss results.

Yes, I know that. I have probably stepped on a couple of toes. As a speaker and a person involved in selling services, I also fall into this category. That's why I have to remind myself that working, writing, speaking and selling with character requires me to avoid manipulative and coercive tactics.

When I am facilitating motivational training programs for business leaders, I am often asked where the line lies between dark psychological tactics and ethical influence and persuasion tactics? Some of these people fully acknowledge that they often use these practices or that their organizations require them to use dark practices as part of the company's processes to obtain and maintain customers.

This is truly unfortunate, and although it will lead to short-term sales and revenue, it will ultimately lead to mistrust, poor business practices, poor employee loyalty, and less successful long-term business outcomes.

In order to distinguish between the motivation and persuasion tactics that are dark and those that are ethical, it is important to assess your intent. We must ask ourselves whether the tactics we use are intended to help the other person? It is all right to be wantingto help yourself as well, but if it's only for your benefit, you can easily fall into dark and unethical practices.

The goal should be to have a mutually beneficial or "win-win" outcome. However, you have to be honest and believe that the other person will really benefit. An example of this is a salesperson who believes that everyone will benefit from his product and that his life will be much better for the customer as a result of the purchase. A salesperson with this mentality can easily fall into using dark tactics to move a person to buy and use the "ends justify the means" mentality. This opens the person up to any tactics to make a sale.

We can ask ourselves the following questions in order to evaluate our intentions along with our motivation and persuasion tactics:

What is my goal for this interaction? Who will benefit, and how?
Do I feel good about how I am approaching the interaction?
Am I totally open and honest?
Will this interaction result in a long-term benefit for the other person?
Will the tactics that I use lead to a more trusting relationship with the other person?
Do you really want to be successful in your leadership, relationships, parenting, work, and other areas of life? Then evaluate yourself to determine your current motivation and persuasion tactics. Doing it right will lead to long-term credibility and influence. Doing it wrong (going dark) leads to poor character, broken relationships, and long-term failure because people will eventually see through the darkness and realize your intent.

The Dark Psychology

Arsonist

An arsonist is a person with an obsession with setting fire. These individuals often have a history of development that is filled with sexual and physical abuse. Common traits among serial arsonists is the tendency to be lonely, to have few peers, and to be absolutely fascinated by the setting of fire. Serial arsonists are very ritualistic and tend to display patterned behaviors in their methodologies for setting fires.

Being concerned about setting fire, arsonists often fantasize and fixate on how to plan their fire setting episodes. Once their target is set, some arsonists experience sexual excitement and masturbate while watching. Despite their pathologically ritualistic patterns, the serial arsonist is proud of his actions.

Necrophiliac

, Thanatophilia, necrophilia and necrocoitus all define the same type of unstable person. These are people who have a sexual attraction to dead bodies. The American Psychiatric Association's Diagnostic and Statistical Manual of Mental Disorders classifies necrophilia as a type of paraphilia. Paraphilia is a biomedical word used to describe a person's sexual excitement and fantasty for objects, situations or individuals that are not part of normative stimulation and may cause distress or serious problems to a normal person. Thus, paraphilia of the necrophiliac is the sexual excitement of a deceased person.

Experts who have compiled necrophiliac profiles indicate that they have tremendous difficulty in experiencing the capacity to be intimate with other living beings. For these people, sexual intimacy with a dead body feels safe and secure rather than sexual intimacy with a living human being. In interviews, necrophiliacs revealed a great sense of control when they were in the company of a corpse. A sense of connection is secondary to the primary requirement for perceived control.

Serial killer

A serial killer is a real human predator, typically defined as someone who kills three or more people over a period of 30 days. Interviews with most serial killers have revealed that there is a cooling-off period between each murder. The serial killer's resting period is a perceptual refractory period during which they are temporarily satisfied with their need to cause pain to others.

Criminal Psychology experts have assumed that their motivation to kill is the pursuit of the experience of psychological gratification achieved only through brutality. After the murder, these individuals feel a sense of liberation combined with egotistical power. The experience brings them such gratification that they will want to feel the experience of release and gratification again.

"The phrase 'serial killings' means a series of three or more murders, not less than one of which was committed within the United States, with common features to suggest a reasonable possibility that the crimes were committed by the same actor."

Sexual assault, humiliation, rape and torture are often involved in their murders. Experts at the Federal Bureau of Investigation outlined other motivations in addition to anger, rage, attention-seeking, thrill-seeking, and monetary gain. Serial killers often have similar patterns in their choice of victims, how they kill their targets and methods for disposing of the body. Criminal experts trained in behavioral analysis of concurrent serial killers have noticed a history of significant emotional, social and behavioral pathology. However, serial killers tend to be solitaries who have difficulty engaging in functional relationships.

Here are threeexamples of offenders and offender groups committing abusive and/or violent, bizarre acts that share a common bond of deep psychological deficits with distorted views. These serious psychiatric and personality constructs, which can metastasize their entire being, challenge reason. What about these human predators? How do they socialize and function in their daily lives? These brief profiles speak volumes of the dark nature of the human condition. In addition to sharing mild to severe psychosis, they are all perceptual loners with deep-seated forces governing their decision-making capacity.

The serial arsonist may not attack other people or find gratification to be a human predator, as does the serial killer, but he actually experiences joy and elation from the setting of his fire. In addition to joy, he has a sense of achievement as a result of the devastation he caused. His episodes of setting fire are extremely dangerous, given that it can cause harm to others, but the goal of causing pain or physical harm is not his modus operandi.

For the serial arsonist, the great reward is his sense of pride and distorted perception of a brilliant feat of genius. His perverted sense of achievement sometimes leads him to become sexually aroused, and masturbation ensued. The conduct of the arsonist is reprehensible, illegal and dangerous, but generally does not involve premeditated murder. They live in an abyss of infernal obsession.

Although the necrophiliac does not cause pain to another person or victimize others, his actions are extremely bizarre and lack any sense of logic. The necrophiliac's urge for perceived control is so insidious that he actually develops a sexual attraction to the corpse. Imagine the experience he has. He is sexually intimate with a lifeless body that has no expression and lacks warmth. Most people yearn for intimacy during sexual intercourse, but this is not required by necrophiliac. He is aroused by the experience of total and complete disconnection. Clearly, his mind has entered into a very dark realm.

The serial killer is one of the most despotic characters on the dark side. In movies, court cases and news coverage, serial killers are often the subject of intrigue. The essence of this deviant evil epitome echoes a part of the human psyche that only the serial killer can experience realistically. Just as an alcoholic yearns for his next drink or an opium addict yearns for his next fix, the serial killer becomes addicted to murder.

The serial killer speaks of gratification and a high sense of release once his murder has come to fruition. Unlike a necrophiliac or serial arsonist, the only aim of a serial killer is to extinguish life. For many of these assailants, the sexual excitement of torturing their victims is a common theme. Although it is a common theme, there are other equally disturbing drives that cause them to torture their victims.

These three examples are illustrations of the extent to which humans are going to experience power, pleasure and/or goal attainment. All of the criminal profiles analyzed involve assailants feeling a sense of gratification from their abusive and/or hateful actions. The reality is that these instances are merely basic profiles of four segments of the population of men and women who are involved in criminal, abusive or deviant acts. The extent to which humans go for sexual gratification, perceived control, or financial gain is quite extensive and elaborate.

Before the advent of scientific advances and society's ability to explain deviant human behavior, monsters and demons were thought to be the cause of such chaos. Unable to understand how people could commit these atrocities, metaphysical beings were the only logical explanation. Instead of frightening their neighbors, early civilizations concocted legends and tales of demonic beings. Werewolves, vampires, and ghouls were stalking their prey at night.

Although contemporary society considers itself advanced in its ability to understand the potential of humans to commit violent and heinous acts, it remains elusive to learn how to reduce and/or prevent bizarre and deadly acts committed by humans. Our species is the main group of living organisms to participate in anti-survival actions.

Dark Psychology is both a study of criminal and deviant behavior and a conceptual framework for deciphering the potential for evil in all human beings. This researcher does not claim to have the "holy grail" of defining deviant human behavior, but rather a framework for investigation and further investigation.

Many years ago, when this researcher first became interested in studying forensic and criminal psychology, he argued that aberrant, deviant behaviors had not yet been identified as part of psychiatric illness. With the passage of time and research, intrigue has followed a vast array of theories and explanations as to why humans retain the capacity to prey on other humans.

CHAPTER TWO

PRINCIPLES OF PERSUASION

The most significant aspects of this volume were the "6 Principles of Influence" of Cialdini, which are:

1. Reciprocity;

2. Commitment/consistencies;

3. Social evidence;

4. Office;

5. Links;

6. Scarcity.

More than three decades after the publication of the book, its six principles have also been adapted to Internet marketing, in particular, the conversion rate business.

This makes sense: conversions are all about persuasion. If there is a user visiting your website, you want to turn them into a shopper and then a buyer.

Every little bit of persuasion counts in the world of conversions. Here's how you can use Cialdini's 6 Persuasive Principles to boost conversions.

1. Reciprocity: Give a little something to get a little something in return.

Cialdini's first principle of persuasion implies that human beings are wired to repay favors and debts — to treat others as they have treated us.

The initiative of reciprocity is that people, by nature, feel obliged to grant discounts or concessions to others if they have received favors from the same people. Psychology explains this by stressing that people simply hate to feel indebted to others!

Let's say you're running a popular blog that provides readers with highly actionable and practical information to improve their lives.

Based on the initiative of reciprocity, your blog will make site visitors more likely to feel obliged to buy something from your site, providing you with an eventual conversion.

2. Commitment: People want their faith to be consistent with their values.

The principle of commitment states that human beings have a profound need to be seen as consistent. Once we have committed to someone or something, we are much more likely to fulfill that commitment (hence, consistency).

From a psychological point of view, this can be explained by the fact that people have aligned their commitment with their self-image.

Marketers have figured out how to use this second Cialdini principle to obtain higher conversion rates.

By having site visitors to commit to something relatively small, such as a guide or whitepaper, they increase the likelihood that site visitors will eventually see themselves as customers. This change in self-perception makes it easier to follow up on an offer for a paid product or service.

3. Social Proof: There is nothing like feeling validated on the basis of what others are doing.

Cialdini simply defined social proof as people doing what they see other people doing.

For example, if our colleagues work late, we are more likely to do the same thing. If a particular food shop is always full of people, we are more likely to try it.

We are even more influenced by this principle if:

We are unsure of ourselves.
The people we observe seem to be similar to us.
Social psychology is rich in experiments that illustrate this inevitable human phenomenon, but the classic one is the 1960s elevator experiment:

Basically, whatever the majority of the people in the elevator do, the individual who joins the group will copy.

For example, if the group looks at the back of the elevator, the individual will do the same thing, even if it looks funny. Most people refuse to think or act independently.

4. Authority: You are going to obey me!

Ever wonder why we tend to obey authority figures, even if they are objectionable and ask others to commit objectionable acts? This is human nature!

Accessories, such as uniforms and job titles (e.g., Dr.), infuse the air of authority, making the average person more likely to accept what the person says. You can see this in commercials that use doctors to run their ad campaigns.

5. Liking: The more you like a person, the more you are going to be persuaded by them.

Does it matter if someone is like you? This affects the chances of you being convinced by that individual, according to Cialdini. Welcome to Principle 5 of Cialdini: like. Liking is based on sharing a similar or more superficial interest, such as physical attractiveness.

This principle can be applied to conversations in the following way: a company that wants to boost conversion rates should create a large "About Us" page.

That sounds absurd, but it makes sense to understand that the company's "About Us" page is an opportunity to tell potential buyers about the similarities between their staff and site visitors. Since similarity is the main building block of like, an effective "About Us" page is vital.

6. Scarcity: If you believe that something is in short supply, you want more!

Here we are, at the end of Cialdini's authoritative list of principles of persuasion. The perception of scarcity is that products are more attractive when their availability is limited.

We are more likely to purchase something if we're told that it's the "last one" or that a "special deal" will soon come to an end. In short, we hate to miss out, and that fear is a powerful motivator that encourages us to act quickly.

Persuasion vs. Manipulation

You are heading to the car dealer, ready to purchase the Toyota Highlander in 2012. You know this car is reliable, in your price range, and it is a great fit for your family. This is what you say to the car salesman who greets you at the door and asks what he can do to help you. Instead of taking you to the Highlander, parked a few rows back, he is going over to the 2015 Cadillac Escalade. "It is much better for you and your family! "He says. He goes on to open the car doors and explain all the luxurious amenities.

The car salesman leaves a bad taste in your mouth, and you quickly realize that he does not have your best interest in mind — he only has his best interest in mind. This is how you understand that you are being manipulated as opposed to being persuaded. As the car salesman has this reputation, it is easy to spot the manipulation. That is not always the case; in fact, it is often difficult to tell whether someone is trying to convince or manipulate you. However, it can be done. You just need to know the signs and learn to protect yourself.

Am I Being Persuaded or Manipulated?

As much as we want to trust every person we know and come into contact with, the reality is that people lie, and people are manipulating. It is, therefore, important that you understand the difference between the two and learn to distinguish them. Luckily, there are two relatively simple ways to do this:

1) Look at the potential outcomes.

Caleb Backe, a health and wellness expert at Maple Holistic, says that the key to distinguishing the difference between persuasion and manipulation is to look at the potential outcome: It could be tricky to be able to tell the difference because that person's intent is probably the biggest contributor. The intention isn't something that can always be picked up. It is a fine line, and it is not always obvious. So, if the intent and the process are not clear, you will have to rely on another factor: the results. How is it affecting your life? How do you feel about the person talking to or otherwise communicating with you? Is the result of that person's behavior, either positive or negative? You may find that you have to think a little more long-term, but the answers are there if you really look at yourself.

2) Listen to your gut.

While weighing potential outcomes will certainly help, Licensed Marriage and Family Therapist Eliza Boquin says, The best way to determine whether you are being persuaded versus manipulated is to look at how you feel. If someone is trying to convince us, they will present us with a point of view or options that we may not have considered. They will highlight the benefits of this option and allow you to decide whether it is of value to you. Manipulation, on the other hand, will make you feel guilty, ashamed, scared, or even anxious. Manipulators are self-serving, and do not worry whether the outcome of your choices is in your best interest. Pay attention to how your body feels when you interact. Is your chest tightening up? Do you feel tense? Is your heart racing around? These may be signs that someone is trying to manipulate you. If instead, you feel more open and can see the value of making a decision, then you were most likely to be persuaded.

Protecting Yourself from Manipulators: Stay in Control

If you use the above techniques and feel that you are, indeed, being manipulated, you must remain in charge of the conversation —

otherwise, you are likely to get bogged down in whatever scheme the manipulator is planning. Protect yourself, remember your concerns, and keep your interactions on track. "It's important to keep a conversation about the real issue and the real facts during the manipulation," says Licensed Psychotherapist Whitney Hawkins. Manipulators will often attempt to cloud you with other information.

This is extremely common in cases where there is substance abuse. The reason for this is not that addicts are bad or manipulative people, but they have to be resourceful in order to support their addiction. In order to maintain their addiction, an incredible amount of work is needed. Individuals with substance use disorders slowly become more skilled at covering up their issues and persuading you that there is not one. In order to keep the addiction alive, manipulation becomes necessary and essential.

Hawkins goes on to emphasize the points above, as you can never be too careful: It can be very difficult to spot manipulation. We all want to believe that we can trust the people around us. Trusting your gut is very important. Evaluate whether the decisions you make with this individual are of any benefit to you.

Ethical Persuasion

Ethical persuasion is the inner ability of a human being to treat others with respect, understanding, care and fairness in order to understand himself and the phases of ethical persuasion are:

1. Explore the point of view of the other person.

2. Explain your point of view.

3. Create resolutions.

The ethic of rhetoric is mainly concerned with morality and the ability of a person not to be tempted in certain instances to help themselves by having a negative impact on others, or just as unethical to use persuasion to increase personal gain without the knowledge of the audience. Ethical behavior is important to the human race, is important to the process of persuasion and has an impact on persuasion by changing the process of persuasion and expanding who is responsible for it. It begins with ethics and develops how to communicate successfully and responsibly, and ends with who needs to be accountable in a persuasive exchange. This ethical view of persuasion is more sophisticated, refined and civilized.

Traits of the manipulator

A skilled emotional manipulator can break your self-esteem and even make you question your health.

It is because emotional manipulation can be so destructive that it is crucial for you to recognize it in your life. It is not as easy as you may think because the emotional manipulators are usually very clever.

They start with subtle manipulation and raise the stakes over time, so slowly that you do not even realize it is going on. Luckily, emotional manipulators are easy enough to spot if you know what to look out for.

1. They are undermining your faith in your grasp of reality. Emotional manipulators are unbelievably skilled liars. They insist that the incident did not happen when it did, and they insist that they did or said something when they did not. The trouble is that they are so good that you end up analyzing your own sanity. To insist that whatever caused the issue is a figment of your imagination is an extremely powerful way to get out of trouble.

2. Their actions are never in line with their words. Emotional manipulators are going to tell you what you want to hear, but their actions are another story. They promise their support, but when the time comes to follow through, they act as though your requests are totally unreasonable. They tell you how lucky they are to know you, and then they act like you are a burden. This is just another way to undermine your belief in your own sanity. They make you check reality as you see it and shape your perception according to what is convenient for them.

3. They are experts on the doling out of guilt. Emotional manipulators are masters in leveraging your guilt to their advantage. If you bring up something that bothers you, they make you feel guilty about mentioning it. They make you feel guilty if you do not, for

33

keeping it to yourself and stewing on it. When you deal with emotional manipulators, whatever you do is wrong, and no matter what problems you both have, it is always your fault.

4. They are claiming the role of the victim. Nothing is their fault when it comes to emotional manipulators. It does not matter what they do — or do not — it is someone else's fault. Someone else has made them do it — and, usually, it is you. If you get angry , it is your fault that you have unreasonably high expectations; if they get mad, it is your fault that you upset them. Emotional manipulators have no responsibility for anything bad that happens.

5. They are too much, too soon. Whether it is a personal relationship or business relationship, emotional manipulators always seem to skip a couple of steps. They share too much, too soon — and expect the same thing from you. They portray sensitivity and vulnerability, but it is a trick. The charade is meant to make you feel "special" to be let into their inner circle, but it is also meant to make you feel not only sorry for them but also responsible for their feelings.

6. It is an emotional black hole. Whatever the emotional manipulators feel, they are geniuses in sucking everyone around them into those emotions. If they're in a poor mood, everyone around them knows that. But that is not the worst: they are so clever that not only do they know their mood, they feel it, too. This creates a tendency for individuals to feel responsible for the moods of the manipulator and to have to fix them.

7. They readily agree to help — and perhaps even volunteer — then act like a martyr. The initial eagerness to help quickly morphs into groans, sighs and suggestions that what they agreed to do is a huge problem. If you show reluctance, they are going to turn it around on you, assuring you that, of course, they want to help and that you are just paranoid. The goal is to make you feel guilty, indebted, and perhaps even insane.

8. They are always one-up. No matter what problems you may have, the emotional manipulators are in a worse situation. They are undermining the legitimacy of your complaints by reminding you that their problems are more serious. The message is that you do not have a reason to complain, so just keep quiet.

9. They know all of your buttons, and do not hesitate to push them. Emotional manipulators know your weak spots, and they are quick to use that knowledge against you. If you are unsure about your weight, they will talk about what you're eating or how your clothes fit tightly; if you are worried about an upcoming presentation, they will point out how intimidating and judgmental the visitors are. They are using their awareness of your emotions to manipulate you, not to make you feel better.

Overcoming Manipulation

Emotional manipulators are driving you crazy because their behavior is so irrational. Do not make any mistake about it — their behavior is really against reason, so why are you allowing yourself to respond emotionally to them and get sucked into the mix?

The more irrational and out-of-the-box someone is, the easier it should be for you to get rid of their traps. Quit trying to beat them at their own game. Emotionally distance yourself from them, and approach your interactions with them as if they were a science project (or that you are shrinking them if you prefer that analogy). You don't need to respond to the emotional chaos — only to the facts.

Maintaining an emotional distance requires a sense of awareness. If you do not recognize when it is going on, you cannot stop someone from pushing your buttons. You may get yourself in conditions where you need to regroup and choose the best way forward. That is all right, and you should not be afraid to buy yourself some time to do that.

Most people feel like when they are working or living with someone; they do not have a way to control the chaos. It could not be further from the truth. Once you have identified a manipulator, you will begin to find their behavior more predictable and easier to understand. This is going to equip you to think rationally about when and where you are going to have to put up with them and when and where you are not. You can set boundaries, but you are going to have to do that consciously and proactively. If you let things happen, you are bound to find yourself constantly embroiled in difficult conversations. If you set boundaries and decide when and where you are going to engage a difficult person, you can control a lot of chaos. The only trick is to stick to your weapons and keep the boundaries in place when the person tries to cross them, which they will.

CHAPTER THREE

RECOGNIZE THE TECHNIQUES OF

MANIPULATION

Not only does it set out a massive 20 tactics that toxic people use to get what they want, but it also offers advice about how to combat their manipulations. The excerpts below may seem extensive, but these ten short summaries are actually only a small fraction of the advice around in the complete post.

1. Gaslighting

"Gaslighting is the manipulative tactic that can be described in different variations of three words: 'That did not happen,' 'You imagined it,' and 'Are you crazy?'. "Gaslighting is perhaps the most insidious and manipulative tactics out there because it works to distort and undermine your sense of reality; it eats away at your ability to trust yourself and inevitably disables you from feeling justified in calling out abuses and mistreatment."

How are you able to fight back? "Ground yourself in your reality — writing things down as they have happened, telling a friend or repeating to your support network of your experience can help counteract the gaslighting effect."

2. Projection

You know when toxic individuals claim all the drowsiness that surrounds them is not their fault, but yours? This is called a projection. We all do it a bit, but the narcissists and the psychopaths do it a lot. "Projection is a defense mechanism used to shift responsibility for one's negative behavior and traits by attributing it to someone else," notes Arabi.

That's the solution? "Don't 'project' your sense of compassion or sympathy to a toxic person, nor do you own any of the toxic person's projections," Arabi recommends. "Proposing our own conscience and value system to others has the potential consequence of further exploitation."

3. Generalizations

You said that a co-worker sometimes fails to consider the long-term consequences of certain financial decisions. The Office Psychopath claims that you called him "a loose cannon". You have noticed that the deal might go south if X, Y, and Z conditions occur. Your narcissistic colleague tells the boss that you said the deal was "a disaster."

What's going on there? It was not just that your nemesis did not understand what you said. It's that he or she didn't have any interest in understanding.

"Malignant narcissists are not always masterminds — many of them are intellectually lazy. Instead of taking the time to cautiously consider a different perspective, they generalize anything and everything you say, making broad statements that do not recognize the nuances of your argument or take into account the multiple perspectives that you have paid tribute to," says Arabi, summarizing this argument.

To counter this, "Hold on to your truth and resist generalizing statements by realizing that they are, in fact, forms of illogical thinking in black and white."

4. Moving the Target Positions

"Abuse narcissists and sociopaths are using a logical fallacy known as 'moving the goalposts' to ensure that they have every reason to be forever dissatisfied with you. This is when, even after you have provided all the evidence in the world to validate your argument or have taken action to fulfill your request, they are setting up another expectation of you or asking for more proof," says Arabi.

Do not play the game. "Validate and approve of yourself. Know that you are full and enough, and you do not have to be made to feel deficient or unworthy in any way," Arabi says.

5. Change the subject

Switching conversational themes sounds innocent enough, but in the hands of a master manipulator, a change of subject becomes a means to avoid accountability. "Narcissists do not want you to be accountable for anything on the subject, so they are going to reroute discussions to benefit them," notes Arabi.

This kind of thing can go on forever if you let it, making it impossible to actually get involved in the matter at hand. Try "Broken Record Method" to fight back: "Continue to state the facts without falling into their distractions. Redirect their sense by saying, That's not what I am talking about. Let us stay attentive to the real issue. If they are not interested, go out and spend your energy on something more important."

6. Name-calling

Just because you have been dealing with this one since you have come across your first playground killer does not make it any less destructive (and apparently, it is going all the way up to presidential politics).

Just do not tolerate it. "It is important to put an end to any interaction that consists of naming and communicating that you will not tolerate it," says Arabi. "Do not internalize it: realize that they have resort to name-calling because they are deficient in higher-level methods."

7. Smear campaigning

"When toxic types cannot handle the way you see yourself, they start controlling how others see you; they play martyrdom while you are labeled toxic. A campaign is a pre-emptive strike to slander your reputation and spoils your name.

Sometimes, true evil geniuses will even divide and conquer, pitting two people or groups against each other. Don't let them succeed. "Document any form of harassment," Arabi advises, and make sure you do not rise to the bait, and do not let the horribleness of the person who provoked you allow you to act in just the kind of negative ways they falsely attributed to you.

8. Devaluation

Beware when an individual who seems to love you while aggressively denouncing the last person who held your position. "Narcissistic abusers do this all the time-they devalue their previous partners to their new partners, and eventually the new partner begins to get the same kind of mistreatment as the narcissist's ex-partner," says Arabi. But this dynamic can happen in both the professional and the personal partner realms.

Simple awareness of the phenomenon is the first step to counteract it. "Be wary of the fact that how a person treats or talks about someone else could potentially translate into how they will treat you in the future," Arabi cautions.

9. Aggressive jokes.

The problem is not your sense of humor, it is the hidden intention of that cutting joke. "Covert narcissists enjoy making malicious remarks at your expense. They are usually dressed up as 'simple jokes' so that they can get away with saying terrible things while still their maintaining innocent and cool behavior. Any time you are outraged by an insensitive or harsh remark, you are accused of having no sense of humor, "says Arabi.

Do not let the office abuser make you think it was all innocent fun — it was not.

10. Triangulation

One of the smartest ways in which truly toxic people can distract you from their negativity is by focusing your attention on the supposed threat of another person. This is called triangulation. "Narcissists love to 'report back' falsehoods about what others say about you," Arabi warns. To resist tactics, realize that the third party in the drama is being manipulated as well—he is also another victim.

You can also try "reverse triangulation" or "to gain support from a third party that is not under the influence of the narcissist."

Learn How to Read People Quickly

There are five tips in which you can read someone's mind – or at least take an educated guess – and build better business relationships:

1. Start with the generation of differences

Understanding someone's generation can give insight into how he or she thinks. It is a lens through which they see life, says Miner.

43

"Generational differences are fascinating," she says. "Millennials often hide behind computers and talk their minds through Twitter and blogs. They do not value face-to-face communication. Boomers like to talk to someone in person."

Miner says understanding a person's generation will help you know the best way to get closer to them in order to develop a relationship. "If we are going to close a millennial deal, we know there is no need to fly out and schedule a roundtable," she says. "They prefer an Internet presentation. For boomers, we are going to spend the money and get out."

Generations also value different things, says Miner. Millennials, for example, are looking for quick results. "When we speak to them, we talk about proven processes," she says. "Boomers are more conservative. When we talk to them, we slow down and talk about things like safety and risk."

2. Acknowledge the hot buttons

Another way to tell what someone is thinking is to look for their pain points, which involves asking the best and right questions. Miner says it is important to build a personal bond to get to know what they consider to be important.

"What triggers emotion for them? Where are the comfort zones? "He asks. "You need a big ear and a small mouth."

Miner suggests skipping pre-canned conversations and entering into a relationship as a discussion. "Ask open-ended and crucial questions that allow a person to share their strengths and challenges," Miner says. "Or share stories about what you did for others. Nine times out of ten, people will agree that they have the same issue, which helps you better understand what they need."

3. Consider the personality

It helps to notice and observe personal qualities to determine who they are and what is important to them.

Miner says she is very analytical and evaluative, and she relates well when people methodically lay down their ideas: "I have taught my team that they have to come to me ready to back up their initiative with numbers," she says. "You have lost me if you do not."

Look for clues about someone's personality by paying attention to the characteristics and the verbiage. Someone who prefers to be dominant might have an overly firm handshake, Miner says. People who welcome humor insert sarcasm into the conversation. Use these steps to determine their values and approach.

4. Look for non-verbal communication

Non-verbal behavior is also important, and Miner suggests looking for hints of body language. If someone leans in, they are engaged. If they back away, look down or turn away, they are not relating to what you are saying.

It is important to build a good ear that can listen to subtle sounds.

The tone of voice can provide clues as well. For example, if someone answers you in monotone, they are most likely unattached and not interested in your concept. If they look at you when you talk and move closer, they find value in what you say.

5. Be a Good Listener

In the end, listen to what someone says and what they are not saying. While this is more difficult when the conversation is over the phone, Miner says that a committed or passionate voice is obvious. It is also obvious when someone is frustrated.

"Their tone changes or you can hear a sigh," she says. "It is crucial to develop a good ear that can listen to subtle sounds."

Anything critical or emotional should never be communicated by email, says Miner. "Pick up your phone," she says. "Emails are awful for conveying the meaning behind the words. They could be a real hindrance to being perceptive."

The Machiavellian

Machiavellian is sneaky, cunning, and lacks a moral code. The term comes from the Italian philosopher Niccolò Machiavelli, who wrote the political treatise The Prince in the 1500s, which encourages "end justifies means" behavior, especially among politicians.

Machiavellian describes the fans of Machiavelli, the Renaissance philosopher who wrote things like "It is much safer to be feared than loved" and "If a man's injury has to be done, it should be so severe that his vengeance does not have to be feared." Modern psychiatrists use it to describe a type of personality disorder, a cold egotism. When Machiavelli's first works were published, some saw them as dangerous and amoral, and the word Machiavelli was coined.

The Narcissist

Narcissistic personality disorder — one of several categories of personality disorders — is a mental condition in which people have an inflated sense of their own importance, a deep need for excessive attention and admiration, troubled relationships, and a lack of sympathy for others. However, behind this mask of extreme trust lies a fragile self-esteem that is vulnerable to the slightest criticism.

Narcissistic personality disorder causes issues in many areas of life, such as relationships, work, school, and financial affairs. People with a narcissistic personality disorder may generally be unhappy and disappointed when they do not receive special favors or admiration that they believe they deserve. They may find their relationships unfulfilling, and others may not enjoy being around them.

People who have narcissistic personality disorder may not want to think anything might be wrong, so they may not be likely to seek treatment. If they seek treatment, they are more likely to have symptoms of depression, drug or alcohol use, or other mental health problems. But perceived self-esteem insults may make it difficult to accept and follow up with treatment.

If you recognize parts of your personality that are common to narcissistic personality disorder, or feel overwhelmed by sadness, consider contacting a trusted doctor or mental health provider. Getting the right treatment can make your life more rewarding and enjoyable.

Psychopath

Psychopaths have the image of a cold, heartless, inhuman being. But do all psychopaths show a complete lack of normal emotional capacity and empathy?

Psychopathy is categorized by diagnostic features such as high intelligence, superficial charm, poor judgment and lack of experience, pathological egocentricity and inability to love, lack of remorse or shame, impulsivity, grandiose self-esteem, pathological lying, manipulative behavior, poor self-control, promiscuous sexual behavior, juvenile delinquency, and criminal behavior. However, do all the Psychopaths show a complete lack of normal emotional capacity and empathy?

Like healthy people, many psychopaths love their parents, their spouses, their children, and their pets in their own way, but they have difficulty in loving and trusting the rest of the world. Psychopaths also suffer emotionally as a result of separation, divorce, death of a loved one, or dissatisfaction with their own deviant behavior.

Sources of Sadness

Psychopaths may suffer from emotional pain for a variety of reasons. Psychopaths, like anyone else, have a deep desire to be loved and cared for. However, this desire often remains unfulfilled, as it is evident that it is not easy for another person to get close to a person with such repellent personality characteristics. Psychopaths are periodically aware of the effects of their behavior on others and can be truly saddened by their inability to control it. The lives of most psychopaths are devoid of a stable social network or of warm, close ties.

Psychopathic life stories are often characterized by chaotic family life, lack of parental attention and guidance, parental substance abuse and antisocial behavior, poor relationships, divorce, and adverse neighborhoods. They may feel that they are prisoners of their own etiological determination and believe that, compared to normal people, they have fewer opportunities or advantages in life.

Despite the arrogance, psychopaths feel inferior to others and know that they are stigmatized by their own behavior. Some psychopaths have superficially adapted to their environment and are even popular, but they feel that they must carefully hide their true nature because it will not be acceptable to others. This leaves the psychopath with a difficult choice: to adapt and participate in an empty, unreal life, or to adapt and live a lonely life isolated from the social community. They see the love and friendship that others share and feel dejected, knowing that they will never be part of it.

Psychopaths are known to need excessive stimulation, but most foolish adventures end in disillusionment due to conflict with others and unrealistic expectations. In addition, many psychopaths are disheartened by their inability to control their sensation-seeking and repeatedly confronted with their weaknesses. Although they may attempt to change, a low response of fear and associated failure to learn from experience lead to repeated negative, frustrating, and depressive confrontations, including problems with the justice system.

As psychopaths age, they are unable to continue their energy-consuming lifestyle and become burnt-out and depressed as they look back on their restless life full of interpersonal discontent. Their health deteriorates as the effects of their recklessness accumulate.

Emotional Pain and Violence

Social isolation, loneliness, and associated emotional pain may precede violent criminal acts. They believe that the world is against them and will eventually become convinced that they deserve special privileges or rights to fulfill their wishes. As the psychopathic serial killers Jeffrey Dahmer and Dennis Nilsen have said, violent psychopaths ultimately reach a point of no return, where they feel they have cut through the last thin connection with the normal world. Subsequently, their sadness and suffering increased, and their crimes became increasingly bizarre.

Dahmer and Nilsen said they killed simply for the company. Both men had no friends, and their social contacts were occasional encounters in gay bars. Nilsen watched the television and talked for hours with the dead bodies of his victims; Dahmer consumed parts of the bodies of his victims in order to become one with them. He believed that his victims were still living in his body in this way.

For the rest of us, it is unbelievable that these people were so lonely, yet they described their loneliness and social failures as indescribably painful. Each of them created his own sadistic universe to avenge his experiences of abuse, rejection, humiliation, neglect, and emotional suffering.

Dahmer and Nilsen said that they did not enjoy the act of killing. Dahmer tried to make the zombies of his victims by injecting acid into their brains after they had been numbed with sleeping pills. He wanted complete control of his victims, but when that failed, he killed them. Nilsen was much more comfortable with dead bodies than with living humans as the dead could not leave him. He wrote good poems and spoke tender words to the dead bodies, using them for the company as long as possible. In other violent psychopaths, a relationship has been found between the intensity of sadness and loneliness and the degree of violence, imprudence and impulsivity.

Self-destruction

Violent psychopaths are at high risk of targeting their aggression towards themselves as well as towards others. As a result of their own behavior (e.g., as a result of risky driving or involvement in hazardous situations), a significant number of psychopaths die a violent death relatively soon after they are discharged from forensic psychiatric treatment. Psychopaths may feel that all life, including their own, is worthless.

Treatment

In the last decade, neurobiological explanations have become available for many of the features of psychopathy. An abnormal level of neurochemicals, including monoamine oxidase (MAO), serotonin and 5-hydroxy indole acetic acid, triiodothyronine, free thyroxine, testosterone, cortisol, adrenocorticotropic hormone, and hypothalamic-pituitary-adrenal and hypothalamic-pituitary-gonadal axes, may determine impulsivity, imprudence, irresponsibility, hostility, and aggressiveness.

Other features, such as sensation-seeking and inability to learn from experience, may be cortical under excitement. It is extremely important to identify hidden suffering, loneliness, and lack of self-esteem as a risk factor for violent, criminal behavior in psychiatrists. Studying the statements of violent psychopaths' sheds light on their striking and specific vulnerability and emotional pain. More experimental psychopharmacotherapy, neurofeedback and combined psychotherapy research are needed to prevent and treat psychiatric behavior.

The Daily Sadist

First of all, when I say "everyday sadist," I do not mean the fun bedtime BDSM kind of sadism that might fit into those two words at first glance. A sadist on a daily basis is a type of personality in which the individual seeks out and acts on opportunities to be cruel. You know they will be throwing a Coke can at the back of your head when you are driving home from work. They are all over the place, but in terms of psychology, they remain somewhat unrecognized.

There is a type known as the Dark Triad of Personality Characteristics, which includes narcissism and psychopathy, as well as what is known as Machiavellianism, a kind of ultra-selfishness defined by "duplicity and cunningness." These are not diseases on their own; they are related behaviors that could be a factor in the diagnosis of something greater and treatable, such as the antisocial persona. You are not likely to win an insanity plea for a diagnosis of Machiavellianism.

An interesting and rather dark study from the University of British Columbia last month suggested the need to upgrade the classification of "daily sadism" to the Dark Triad ranks. Essentially, the research has shown that sadistic behavior can be "captured" or predicted in an experimental setting. One part of the work provided participants (unknowing that they were evaluated as sadists) with a sadism questionnaire (asking things like, "Do you agree that hurting people is exciting?") and then offered participants different options for a task to complete: grinding live bugs in a machine, helping someone grind bugs, cleaning toilets, or holding their hands in ice water. Yes, social psychology is pretty amazing.

The findings are clear: the sadists on paper were sadists in real life. Or they thought they were sadists; the bugs were actually spared, unknown to the participants. Meanwhile, in the second part of the study, sadists from the first part were given the opportunity to blow white noise at other humans for kicks, but only after completing a boring, tiring task. Those high on the sadistic questionnaire thought it was worth the trouble, while those high on the other side of the Dark Triad could not be bothered. "Only sadists were willing to work for an opportunity to hurt an innocent person," explains the study. This implies that sadism is something separate from the other Dark Triad behaviors.

"We hope that this research will persuade readers to interpret sadism as something more than a sexual disorder to be studied in hardened criminals," the researchers, led by EE Buckles, said in a press release, which is a statement that really only reinforces how incredibly strange this whole realm of psychology makes me feel good and that I probably need to work even harder to avoid other humans.

CHAPTER FOUR

DARK TECHNIQUE

Everyone has heard the great tales of the dark side of hypnosis, the stories of suspense, murder, heartbreak or cold heart-felt revenge. This stuff entertains all of us in the modern world. The dark side of hypnosis is often talked about in books, movies, and TV. Is there a dark side to the hypnosis? Actually, there is a kind of thing, but the dark side of hypnosis is a lot more boring than the entertainment industry would have liked you to believe. In fact, a large part of the dark side of hypnosis is played by the entertainment industry as well as many other parts of everyday life.

Now we have discovered (at least those of you who followed the series) that hypnosis is going on all the time. Most of the time is spent in and out of hypnotic trances without even realizing that this is happening. We can often be hypnotized by mistake, but those kinds of moments are usually harmless and unnoticed. Sometimes, we can be targeted for a purpose. Advertising is a powerful example, and successful salespeople often use hypnotic techniques to convince others to buy.

As you may be aware, the main organizations using hypnotic techniques are the media, government, advertising, radio and television. Give yourself a minute to remember a time when there was no TV and you will recall people living with little more than they need. They are usually pretty happy on their own without the television bombarding them with messages about all the things they need. Compared tothe present, which is a completely different reality.

Thousands of subliminal messages convince us every day to buy larger, more imaginative things. Email instead of regular mail. Throw away nappies instead of cotton ones. For this reason, I do not watch a lot of TVs. Do you think I have never seen Pop Idol before? Adverts are created for a lot of purposes. The omission is to encourage you to buy something, something they think they can convince you that you need it. The media can be pretty nasty with their ability to influence us. How often do you see a happy, fun story in the news? It is all about what brings the best ratings!

Unfortunately, it always seems to be the sad, negative stories on the front page. Think about it, how many people would actually be watching the news if all that was reported were positive stories. It says a lot about who we think we are.

The worst thing about this dark side of hypnosis is that it creates a negative illusion about our world. Yes, sometimes it is good to know that bad things are going on around us so that we can learn to stop them from happening. It is stupid, however, to think that the news we are receiving is all that is going on in the world. Basically, many of us have been made to behave like fools because of the hypnotic techniques that the media uses against us. Hypnosis has a lot of power, and it is vital that we take these dangers into account in an environment full of subliminal messages and suggestions.

However, these techniques will have no power against you as you become more aware of them. The more you learn about the different techniques that are used against you, the more power you will have over your own life, and the less you will be influenced by the dark side of hypnosis.

Discover Deception

The dictionary defines deception as intentionally causing someone to believe something that is not true.

Anyone can practice deception because it is one of the sins of human nature. Deception may appeal to the mind or to emotions. It uses human desire for knowledge or information as bait to tap into the minds or feelings of its victims.

Deception directed toward the mind comes in the form of "knowledge"—knowledge that is untrue or distorted. Deception pointed to emotions-presents a false picture of "good" feelings that would result.

When the body is targeted by deception, it is supposed to perform certain feats at the expense of hidden side effects. The most serious form of deception, however, is that directed toward the human spirit.

This is serious because, ultimately, it can determine one's eternal destiny. Yet, because of deception, too many believe that spiritual matters are of little or no consequence.

Deception of the human spirit is the most serious thing that can happen to mankind. Individuals should pay attention and use the only spiritual weapons at their disposal to combat deception.

The apparent lack of serious concern on the part of some people about the truth; and their eternal destiny; may be due to incredulity; or to the receipt of incorrect information. However, it is the duty of the individual to align himself with the Truth-to place him or herself on the right side of eternity!

When it comes to the truthfulness of a person — or lack of it— rationalization is usually at work when they try to cover up what they do not want you to know. Here is a little piece of reality. Deception comes naturally to people. They have all done it, and everyone has done it to them. It is a self-preservation technique, ready to take us out of any jam at a moment's notice.

Another trait most of us share? Rationalization. Typically, we are going to find a way to do what we want to do. It seems like the only sensible thing to do. We rationalize the purchase of a new car-by telling ourselves that the one we drive is untrustworthy because it has too many miles. We rationalize the wrong action towards another person by reminding ourselves of what they have done to us in the past. People tend to find ways to make their actions meaningful, even if only in their own minds.

How does it all relate to deception? Well, rationalization is what facilitates deception and makes it permissible for a deceptive person to think about it. They subconsciously figure out ways to reassure themselves their behavior makes sense, that it's justified. This enables them to:

In the first place, do what they want
Be deceptive when you talk about it
Do not feel guilty
No guilt? Scary but true. Contrarily to what might be popular belief, people feel virtually no guilt when they lie; why would they? They justified their deceit by allowing themselves to do whatever it takes to "protect" them from the discomfort that the truth would bring them.

Their concern is not with the morality of deceit but with its success. So here is an interesting little secret that few know: when you see the nervousness shown by a deceptive person, it is not because of feelings of guilt — it is because of their fear of being caught. Rationalization is a big part of what moves a person down the path of deception, and it actually works on three levels, usually spread out over a stretch of time as things unfold:

1-They rationalize action: people generally find ways to do what they want to do, They justify their actions by making what they want to do appear acceptable to themselves. For example, if there is something we really want to buy, we usually find a way to rationalize it so that we get what we want. We buy what we want, and then we back up that decision with logic.

Example: We want a new car, and so we rationalize the purchase by telling ourselves that we are going to save on maintenance (logic) or get better gas mileage (logic) or that the new car will have more room (logic). An emotional urge backed up by a number of "logical" reasons, all designed to make the action appear to be understandable, permissible, even necessary. In the end, we are just rationalizing why it's reasonable to do what we are trying to do.

In the same vein, when a person wants to do something they are not supposed to do, or that is not acceptable to others, they subconsciously rationalize why it is going to be all right. People do not always make good decisions at a time when no one is looking, or when they think no one is going to find out and these two factors end up leading them to go ahead and do what they are trying to do! Let me ask you (hey, no one will know, so you can be honest): Have you ever done something that seemed enticing or fun at the moment, knowing that it would not be seen so well if others found out about it?

Majority of us have at some point.

2-They rationalize deception: then comes the moment to face up to their actions. Maybe someone accidentally touches the "touchy" subject. Maybe someone is asking directly about it. Either way, a decision has to be made: tell the truth, or use deception to set it aside. People often rationalize their dishonesty when they choose to avoid the truth. They might say that the truth is nobody else's business. Or that the truth cannot be proved, and it will be easier not to address it. Or that the other person would be hurt by the truth. Whatever "logic" they use internally is to justify what they really want to do and what is best for them: avoiding the pain of telling the truth.

3-They are rationalizing to the deceived ... When their "secret" actions are uncovered, and the truth becomes known, a deceptive person will often use rationalization again, this time to minimize their dishonesty or even re-frame it as a misunderstanding.

From fertility to birth, everything is designed and built on a pre-determined program. The basis of creation is reality and facts so that human beings can understand existence and its purpose. Human life progresses and spreads along a straight, and right path with justification as the foundation of truth is laid. The diversion of life leads to disaster if human beings adopt lies and remain in the deceptive realm. It is imperative that we all explore and understand the truth, lies and deception.

Truth is defined as, "The state of being in accord with a particular fact or reality. It is in accord with the body of real things, events or actualities." Many scholars and philosophers continue to debate various theories of truth; their logical, factual and ethical meanings.

However, its literal and structural meaning is to express, at the same time, the executions of facts in action and deeds. In this materialistic society, therefore, it is expressed as a bitter pill. On the other hand, its inherent value is bliss and satisfaction.

The world has witnessed, on many occasions, the reward it bestows on true people. Their words are recognized as the truth of the Gospel. These people are called trustworthy. An authentic but undisputed fact is that telling the truth restricts one's actions and actions to the facts. However, lies repeatedly cover up and justify falsehood. We, therefore, need to explore the meaning of lies and their effects.

A lie is defined as a false statement made with a deliberate intention to deceive. It is also intentional falsehood. The definition is self-explanatory and needs no emphasis. However, the reasons, circumstances and situational demands make it necessary for individuals to commit themselves to lie. This act will lead to disastrous consequences, resulting in the tainting of the image and the collapse of the system.

Discussion of lies may be technically justified in favor of a person telling lies, depending on his own concept. Consequently, it will give a temporary recess and defeat. Finally, the facts will emerge and reveal the trustworthiness of the person. Situational lies may seem logical, and the aura of deception still prevails in a disguised form.

Deception is closely linked to lies and finely woven within its concept and meaning. Thus, "Deception is a major relational transgression that often leads to feelings of betrayal and distrust between the relational partners. Deception violates relational rules and is considered to be a negative violation of expectations "(Reference: Wikipedia). Motivation is the main cause of deception. It could be between two individuals or groups and nations. The variance of deception can be romantic, cultural, corporate and political. The aim is to camouflage the motive and present it as an acceptable solution to achieve the ultimate goal.

There is a marked difference between truth alone and the bias of truth. When truth becomes a bias, presenting a relational transgression at the expense of the factuality of events, then lies and deception becomes a camouflage. Therefore, it is advisable to restrict ourselves or adhere to the core concept of truth within its sanctity.

Detection of Deception through Non-Verbal Communication

You can detect deception in non-verbal communication. It may be a bit subtle for someone who is verbally deceitful, but it is still recognizable. Listed below are the main ways in which you can detect deception through non-verbal communication.

Avoidance

This is the most obvious way to tell if a person is lying to you about something. They will just avoid direct contact with you. If this is a spouse/girlfriend/boyfriend, they will start working till a later time. You will find that all of a sudden, their social calendar is booked, and private times are getting less and more difficult. When they are pressed for direct contact, they will still try to avoid getting in touch with you.

Avoidance is the easiest way for someone to be deceptive and not to have to deal with what they have done on a direct level. Even though they know what they have done, avoidance is the easiest way to postpone having to deal with the issue(s) at hand.

Lack of Physical Affection

This is a fairly common issue when someone in a committed relationship is having an affair. The guilt that the unfaithful person has resulted in his rejection of the other person physically, which may result in a lack of hugging, intimate physical relationships, lack of hand-holding, or insistence on personal body space.

If you are used to greeting friends and family members with hugs and or kisses, and all of a sudden, it stops. This suggests a very obvious non-verbal communication. A change in this behavior suggests anger or sudden indifference.

When we're troubled with deception, our general inclination is to physically push people away. That is especially true when it is the person to whom we are deceitful to.

Being Suddenly Secretive

A very noticeable detection of non-verbal deception is sudden secrecy. You notice someone near you suddenly hiding things from you. It might be bills that they do not want you to see the charges on. It might be their use of the internet. It might be emails that they are hiding. There might be text messages that they do npt want you to see. You might notice new password protection on the computer or cell phone.

Detecting this form of non-verbal deception may take time to notice because it is not necessarily initially obvious. However, if you find one sign of this type of deception, it is possible that there will also be other clues to follow.

Detecting deceptive non-verbal communication is sometimes easier than others. One thing to keep in mind is that, as a human race, we have a need to express ourselves. If we do not do this verbally, we are likely to do it non-verbally. Deception is usually based on guilt, lies and half-truths. Holding this in is not easy and very disturbing.

CHAPTER FIVE

HANDLING

Handling is a simple matter of dealing with stressful situations. Stress can become an even bigger problem during the holiday season. With the added tasks of shopping for gifts, preparing food for many people, and dealing with friends and family members, stress levels in your body can build up to a dangerous level.

In case of an emergency, our bodies need to feel stress. This goes all the way back to our caveman days when we were forced to flee wild animals and seek food and shelter on a daily basis in life-threatening situations.

Those days are over. Our present life may be rushed and full of activities, but our lives are rarely at risk. Now we need to focus on staying calm and feeling more relaxed every minute we can. This keeps your blood pressure down to a safe level and can also prevent you from getting old prematurely. It is worth investigating a number of ways to reduce or eliminate stress from your life.

Meditation is a great way to calm and de-stress your whole mind and body. It is going to take time to get used to calming your mind, so you need to start doing it for just a few minutes at a time. After a few weeks of practicing this, you will be able to meditate for longer periods of time.

If you have a family situation that is particularly stressful, sit down and discuss it honestly with your family members so that they know how serious the stress can be. This will help them to be more understanding and supportive if you need some quiet time for yourself.

Using Meditation to Handle Stressful Situations

Stress has gone from being a problem to a pandemic. Kids feel stressed at school, hoping to get good grades, impressing the right people and feeling nervous about the future. Adults are concerned about jobs, inflation and many events around the world. What the hell can you do?

It is not always going to be the right answer to take medication. Herbs may also cause somnolence problems, make you sluggish, and may not be strong enough. There has got to be another answer, and there is.

The Easterners call it meditation. What I am using is probably similar, and whatever your background is, it might be useful. I call it imagery, using an ingrained, memorized set of phrases that can calm you down. As a Christian, I look at the Bible, and it has some very useful passages for this purpose. The first example is the 23rd Psalm.

The Lord is my Shepherd, I will not want:

Everything I need is going to be provided. I am not going to need anything and when I need it; it is going to be there. As an adult, I have no childlike faith in my parents. They could do all things when I was young. Now, it is a bit harder, but the first part of this picture is putting me back there.

It takes me to rest in the green pastures:

Sheep are anxious creatures, and they need to be taken to peaceful places to graze. Without the Shepherd, they are too anxious to eat. The ancient shepherds would carefully lead the flocks to peaceful, green pastures. No loud noise, no sudden movements, basically nothing that would cause alarm. In a world full of alarms, sirens, stress, and hectic pace, what we need is a quiet place to retreat. We need a place, even if it is only in our minds, that we can be at peace.

He Brings Me to Still Waters:

I grew up beside a creek, and the gentle, lapping sound of softly moving water often gave me a lullaby that I cannot find in the desert of SoCal. However, my imagery can place me in the green pasture next to the still water. Just imagining this lowered my blood pressure from dangerous to normal at least once.

When I go through the deepest darkness, I am not afraid of the evil:

There are two things to see here. One of them is the ancient shepherds. Have you ever wondered why they had the funny looking staff? They were known as Shepherd's crook, and the curve was of definite use. Any sheep that fell into a crevasse had to be lifted to survive. That handy, dandy crook would lift them out of most of these dangerous situations. For my imagery, I am thinking of being protected by someone who could defeat any enemy. No one could harm me. There are other comforting passages in this Psalm and in many others. For example, "I am going to lift my eyes to the hills, from where my help comes."

Look for the peace of your passages. Find things you can memorize that will make you feel comfortable in a bad situation. Imagine yourself in that situation when you do. Find something that makes you feel loved, cared for and comforted. If you do not know where to begin, the Psalms are a good start.

Stop the Foreclosure

When it comes to the foreclosure process, you can end up completely losing your home. So, yes, the feeling is not going to be a good one, but it is one that you can use to your advantage. Tap on that frustration and build a defense like no one has ever seen before. It is probably your only chance to stop the foreclosure.

Usually, banks like to take real estate as collateral for the loan they are giving you. That is probably why your home is about to be foreclosed right now. If you are going to stop them from taking it away from you, you are going to have to look for something else to give it. You work that out with your lawyer.

For money loaned, you should expect to have to pay up your mortgage. If you find that you cannot, you are going to face foreclosure, and then you are going to have to deal with trying to stop it. This is not a particularly interesting prospect, but one that a few have achieved in the past. If you tried very hard, you could be the next jewel on that crown.

You are the mortgagor, and you get to retain possession of your property if you do not get foreclosed. If you fail to pay, though, they will serve you with the papers, and you will either lose the property; otherwise, you will fight, and you will just win.

Stopping foreclosure is a full-time job, not something you do on and off. You might not be the attorney doing all the hard legwork, but a lot of what you have to do will involve following up with them and asking to see the details of their progress. Your chances lie in your ability to spot the problems as they arise and address them.

Making the Most of It-Managing Difficult Situations

Life can be a difficult situation; life can also be an easy situation. It is always for certain that it is always a situation to make the most of. To make life and existence a good thing, you must have a certain amount of total flexibility and adaptability, and it must be high, not low. High degrees of flexibility, adjustable attitude and adaptability are the keys to ensuring that wherever you want to go you go like a guided missile, it reaches its targets in the same way, only in a positive way, life and existence that confirms its meaning and way.

All situations require a certain amount of adaptability, adaptation and flexibility, easy or hard, good or bad, wonderful or awful, to be successful. Failure is always certain with rigidity. Understanding only creates success when the right method is used. If you save comprehension for "the right time," that is the sure way to fail. Indeed, any time is or maybe the right time to use what you really have within you to actually achieve what you want and need.

Stand Tall for Your Belief

Do not attempt to influence any person of your beliefs; escaping the financial stress will not occur.The stronger your beliefs, the stronger obstacles will come and try to shut your dreams down. Levels that may be climbed and every level reached, there are new struggles that one must conquer. Your wings are growing.

Ever stopped and looked at a caterpillar turn into a butterfly? How free and beautiful a butterfly flies gracefully and effortlessly. The journey of the butterfly did not begin that way.

Do not let past circumstances shape your financial journey. Situations will always be there. There will always be disappointments. How situations are handled depends on one's own thinking.

In order to succeed, one must move towards the life of a butterfly, taking the risk and fluttering wings where the wind carries them. Many times, people ask others about the direction of their life's financial journey. Why do people think that other people know them better?

Everyone has got an inner voice. People should stop for a moment, get in their dark corner, and listen to their inner voice of reason. That voice will guide you in standing and then move your faith towards the beautiful life of a butterfly, full of financial freedom. Your voice of reason is preparing for the victorious good things that are coming.

The first step is to believe in oneself. There is no way to fake it.

Need to Escape Financial Stress

It is time to stop being scared. By looking at the mirror, there are two choices.

1. Stay right where you are or
2. Move your feet and get out of the dead-end financial situation. People feel that their cocoon is their protection, their bubble against a harsh or unfriendly environment. This cocoon hinders peace, security, and the need to escape financial stress.

Belief Teaches How to Fly

Ever sat back and wondered why. Why did he have to fly to the moon? Why did he make the light bulb? Why did he make it a great way to be a talk show host? Why is he making so much money? Why did they choose to create Facebook, Microsoft or Tennis shoes? Why? Why? Why? Faith was the only thing they had in themselves. Their faith in their cause, their belief in their product, and their perseverance.

Faith causes a person to be determined. The others are sleeping when they work. When others eat, they eat while they' ae working. They let their faith lead them to freedom. They stepped out of their financial cocoon, spread their beautiful butterfly wings, flew into their glorious financial destination, and escaped financial stress. Belief gives the ability not to look left or right. Keep looking straight ahead, and move forward to fly.

Life is a Journey

Get a piece of paper. Write down your name and the date. Write down your strengths on the left. On the right, write down your weaknesses. Be honest with yourself. This is the first way towards healing, the first step towards growth. Look at the weaknesses, then go to the book store and read about how to eliminate the weaknesses.

Individuals are the only ones who can change and make a difference in their journey of life. If the finances are not at the desired figure, stop trying to point your finger at someone else or past circumstances. It is the period to move out of your own way.

If you are not strong enough to believe in yourself, let your faith in the vision of the family carry you. Believe in going to grow beautiful wings for an incredible life; to escape financial stress.

CHAPTER SIX

BRAINWASHING/MIND CONTROL

There are ways of brainwashing you that are covert, repetitive, and very effective. You are probably getting brainwashing without your knowledge right now. These techniques are the reason you are overweight; you smoke, you have pain, you cannot sleep, along with most of your shortcomings.

You have been receiving messages all throughout life that has made you doubt your own thoughts, beliefs, and perceptions. This is happening all time, and it has become a fundamental process of human communication. These patterns of communication are most often used for the benefit of another party. However, if you recognize these techniques in action, you can stop them before they further harm you.

Most of these techniques are so effective that the recipient willingly reassesses what they see. However, these techniques can also be very powerful, symbolically demanding that the recipient changes their perception.

Questioning Brainwashing

One of these covert brainwashing techniques is in the form of questioning. Repeated questioning, organized in a precarious pattern, will cause the subject to analyze things that they did not even think about. As this process proceeds, the subject unknowingly follows through until there is a state of confusion as to the original thought or experience. The end result could be a new memory, a new thought or a new way of thinking.

Here is what happens when you are questioned by a skilled person. Each time a question is asked, you may respond with subtle variations of a story or memory. This skilled practitioner, an advertiser, or an authority figure may eventually cause you to doubt your own thinking. The longer this process, the more it repeats itself, the less you recognize the pattern, the more effective the outcome. You do not know what you think or have experienced before you know it, and the more you agree with the message, the advertisement or authority representation of the information. You have just been brainwashed!

Pay Attention and Acknowledge Brainwashing

If you pay attention to the news, advertisers, authority figures, you will begin to notice this form of brainwashing. Some individuals are so skilled at these techniques that they use it as a standard form of communication.

If you are innocent, you are going to be a victim. It is vitally important to be on guard with these techniques. You need to know that you are under constant assault. If you do not, it will not be long before you do not have the original idea. You will no longer have discerning processes of thought. You are no longer in charge of your life. You are going to think you are going to do, you are going to buy, you are going to follow, and you are going to be one of the many brainwashed. And you are not ever going to realize it!

You are going to need to question everything. If you are overweight, if you cannot stop smoking, if you are in pain, if you are up at night with insomnia, your brain is racing, preventing you from sleeping, if you have any condition that someone else can benefit from, that condition has been created, and only you can reverse it.

Mind control brainwashing techniques can be useful when used ethically but can be dangerous in the wrong hands.

While some people use them for self-development purposes, others have no qualms about using them to harm you. Do not let yourself be manipulated. Read on to learn more about these methods!

Mind Control Brainwashing Technique # 1:

Hypnosis No Permission

A lot of individuals are turning to hypnosis to help them remember childhood memories and past lives. Sometimes they look at hypnosis to help them change something about themselves.

There is nothing wrong with seeking alternative treatment. In fact, many have proclaimed how life changing hypnotic sessions could be.

The danger lies in putting yourself in the hands of a hypnotherapist you do not know about. You may unwittingly endanger your life and well-being.

When someone comes up to you and says, he or she can put you in a trance, do not let that person try, even if you believe in the power of hypnosis. You will need to be supported by a person you trust.

Mind Control Brainwashing Technique # 2: Isolated from Family

One of the most sinister methods of brainwashing is isolation. This is when you are separated from your family, friends, and all familiar things forcibly.

You may not think of it as a big deal, but being isolated from everyone else can have a dramatic effect on your psyche. Social isolation does not just strip you of your personal thoughts; it also moulds you into whatever the person or group of people wants you to think about.

With no one else to support you, you would not have a choice but to go along with the popular thoughts. To avoid being brainwashed like this, be on the lookout for people who insist on driving you away from family and friends.

Mind Control Brainwashing Technique # 3: Scare Tactics Playing with Your Mind

Scare tactics can be anything from a threat to cryptic mind games. This mind control trick feeds on the fear of a person and is, without doubt, one of the most dangerous of all.

If you feel threatened in any way, it is important that you seek the help of your friends, your family and the right authorities. Paranoia alone can make you do something that you would not normally do in normal circumstances.

These brainwashing techniques for mind control are almost invisible in nature. However, with awareness and proper support, you can now defend yourself against people who use them unethically and keep you out of danger.

Steps of Brainwashing in Anorexia

I have analyzed the brainwashing steps above in relation to eating disorders, and here's what I've come up with:

1. Identity Assault: when anorexia begins after an emotional event or a number of emotional events, the anorexic begins to think that they are not who they should be and who they want to be. A person is under constant self-identity attacks for days, weeks, or months, to the point that he is exhausted, confused, and disoriented. In this

state, their beliefs seem to be less solid. They are looking around for a substitute for their identity.

2. Guilt : Constant thoughts: "You are bad the way you are." They feel their body is disgusting; they feel disgusted by their own body. When the growth of anorexia coincides with the time of puberty, thoughts of being ashamed of one's own body are associated with feelings of disgust about sex and intimacy, and this may have dramatic consequences. Associations of guilt and shame about intimacy and sex can end up being a life sentence for many sufferers unless major changes are initiated later in life.

Eating can also be associated with guilt, and this is a major reason why anorexia is turning into bulimia at a later stage of the disease for some sufferers. People start to feel a general sense of shame that all they do is wrong.

Many researchers have reviewed that feelings of guilt are closely linked to the development of eating disorders (especially bulimia and binge eating).

3. Self-betrayal: This is when anorexia starts telling himself, "Agree with me that you are bad." Once a person is confused and drowned in guilt, those thoughts force him to withdraw from his family, friends and peers who eat normally and enjoy their lives. This betrayal of his own trust in themselves and the people close to them increases the shame and loss of identity that the person is experiencing.

4. Breaking point: The victim is constantly asking himself, "Who am I, where am I, and what am I supposed to do?" At this point, the person has his identity in crisis, experiencing profound shame and guilt. Also, a person may undergo a "nervous breakdown," which may involve uncontrollable sobbing, deep depression, and general disorientation and withdrawal. Not all of them have the same severity of symptoms, but many people have this exact reaction.

5. Leniency: Anorexia then tells the patient: "Follow me - I can help you." Anorexic people believe that their anorexia is the only way they can live. Performing anorexic behavior like starvation, purging, brings temporary relief to their feelings, though short-lived. However, more and more attention is required until a person is 100 percent consumed by their distorted anorexic thoughts and feelings.

6. Confession compulsion: "I can help myself."

For a start in the brainwashing process, the anorexic person is confronted with a contrast between guilt and identity pain and a feeling of sudden relief and leniency. A person may feel a desire to talk to other people with the same problems and visit 'thinspiration' sites. (Sites that are set up by other victims to try and justify their inability to deal with their anorexia in the real world.) They may begin to share their experiences of anorexia, provide advice to each other on the best diet, vomit-inducing tricks, compete for the biggest loser.

7. Channeling of guilt: That's why you are in pain. After weeks or months of suffering, breakdown, confusion and moments of leniency, the person's guilt has lost all meaning and numbness replaces it all. It creates something of a blank slate that lets anorexia go deeper and deeper into the soul. Anorexia attaches itself to the person's guilt and belief system as opposed to healthy people.

It is the stage when anorexic people begin to show bad tantrums when parents try to feed them or persuade them to eat and stop their abnormal behavior. They begin to believe that anorexia is not a disease but that it is a lifestyle and that they associate their own self with anorexia: they become one with the disease.

8. Releasing of guilt: it is not me; it is my belief. With his full confession, the person has completed his psychological rejection of his former identity. The sufferer has gradually given up all his formerly enjoyable activities, left his job or college. All this is just for the sake of practicing anorexic lifestyle.

9. Progress and Harmony: "If you want, you can choose the right one. say your" thinspiration "friends.

These "Thinspiration" friends are introducing a new belief system as the path to "good." At this stage, anorexia stops hurting, offering the suffering physical comfort and mental calm in conjunction with their new belief system. People get a "team spirit" attitude with their friends who practice the same dangerous way of life.

10. Final confession and rebirth: their mind is equal to their anorexia, which tells them: "I choose well."

Anorexia is good. The person has no doubt in the righteousness of his choice to be anorexic. It seems impossible at this stage to separate them from anorexia. People continue to practice this dangerous way of life. Thousands of them die as a result of this sooner rather than later. Some may live longer but still eventually die of serious complications or commit suicide as a result of their stasis.

This is how the anorexic mind is programmed (brainwashed) to be the way it suffers from severe anorexia. Most of the eating disorder sufferers go through similar stages, but often these stages happen differently for each patient, and it is difficult to distinguish between them.

Seduction

Seduction is the art of consciously attracting or tempting an individual to engage in sexual activity.

Even if seduction could mean a lot of things apart from sexual activity, the mere fact that the main purpose of seduction is to attract an individual to certain sexual activities makes it even more prone to sexual pleasure.

There are ways that can be used for seduction. One of the most popular is video seduction. Most social behavior experts believe that the mind is stimulated by means of audio and video.

The reason behind this occurrence is that the creation of these two powerful means of technology can create motivation based on psychological manipulation and recall rather than the use of persuasive power, logical influences, or money.

Somepeople have excellent seduction skills, but they still use seduction videos as a medium for disseminating messages.

Meeting an individual and generally trying to have a particular effect on that individual creates anxiety for most people, both for those just starting to date and those more experienced in the dating field. Something triggers the hormones in your body into sudden overdrive, but it is what you do after this trigger that counts. Some people, even after the initial contact with the opposite sex, tend to be unsure.

Seduction stands for different things in different cultures and different groups of people. While seduction for some people inspires images of love and emotional intimacy and generates a sense of excitement, sensuality and sexual desire, most people do not like the idea of seducing, for many others, the idea of seduction creates a fear of being deceived, victimized and sexually harassed.

Attempts in the last few decades to make our society more sex-positive have only produced a viciously superficial discourse that has further deepened our fear of the art of seduction as if it were freely expressed, that is hurtful, destructive and harmful to us as individuals and to society as a whole.

In our modern society, seduction corresponds to deception, trickery, selfishness, exploitation, pretense and/or play on words. One is seduced by the promise of a lover, a salesman, a politician, or an artist. Seduction seems clearly designed to trick one into taking nonsense from reality. We see this kind of seduction celebrated as entertainment and advertised as a commodity complete with porn.

This disenchanted interpretation of seduction as a desire to act, the body as something that cannot wait to be undressed, has infiltrated even our sexual relations. In most cases, seduction has nothing to do with love or even being attracted to the other person. It is about getting something like sex or financial favors through the use of deceit and trickery.

Most people learn the power of exploitative seduction from a very young age, using seduction to get what they want from their parents and siblings, and special favors from teachers and other children. It begins when a child who is often shy, uncertain and does not feel confident in himself becomes aware that by seducing others, he can get their attention.

As they grow older, they continue this pattern and automatically switch to seduction when they want something from someone. They feel excited when they are able to seduce, but at the core of their being. Their self-esteem depends on whether or not they can seduce others. Seduction feeds their lack of self-esteem and lack of trust.

When we seduce in this way, it is just a false sense of power based on another that allows us to seduce them. When we are exploitatively seduced, we have basically given our power to the seducer. It takes away the naturalness, the truth, and the whole reality of the empowering qualities of the art of seduction. A person in his own personal power, full of self-love and self-worth, has no need to be seduced in a manipulative way, nor can he be manipulatively seduced.

Given that manipulative seduction has permeated our modern world, is a frustrating, superficial, mechanical, predictable, manipulative, selfish, emotionally disconnected relationship, void of passion and heightened intimacy inevitable? Should we raise our hands and never hope to possess the rare transformative well of power, healing and spiritual upliftment that the art of seduction offers?

Of course not! Ancient practitioners of the art of seduction were so amazed at the power of this energy that they were convinced that it was the secret of youth, health and vitality.

Our human nature has not changed so much that we cannot do our part. Indeed, the evolutionary work had already begun. Modern versions of "old rituals and practices" provide modern audiences with insights into what the art of seduction once was, but when we begin to believe that it is the only way to connect with the opposite sex, we fall into the trap of memorized pick-up lines and mechanical seduction scripts that steal from us the very power that makes the art of seduction so naturally powerful. Invariably, we lose both the heart and the soul of the seduction phenomenon and, thus, our connection to one of the deepest and most profound aspects of human fulfillment.

It is time to demystify and rehabilitate the lost art of seduction and use its mega power. The whole mystery of this long-forgotten and long-misunderstood timeless ritual may well be what we need today to save us from the current erotic famine, to get our groove back on and the fire back in our groins.

Defend Yourself from Toxic People

Set the Boundary

Just because you live or work with someone, it does not mean that chaos is out of your control. Be a little more observant and try to notice the predictable behavior of the toxic person. Eventually, you will train your mind to think rationally about whether or not you should deal with them. Boundaries are set proactively and consciously. They help you decide whether to engage a difficult person. Stay alert when handling toxic people, and always be ready to stand up for yourself. Remember, it is all right to say no.

You are controlling your emotions.

Understand that you are in complete control of your emotions. Nobody makes you feel a certain way. That is simply the result of choosing to react that way. If you are being attacked by a toxic person, see if you can be aware of the stress and anger that you feel and be the bigger person. It is very likely that you do not enjoy having negative emotions, so do not let them get the better of you!

Limit Controlled Stress (Caffeine and Sleep)

Did you know that caffeine triggers the release of adrenaline in our bodies? Adrenaline stimulates your fight-or-flight response, which is a survival mechanism designed to either make you fight or run away (good for when wildlife chasing after you, but not so good when you are meeting a classmate or a coworker in the hallway). Instead of rational thinking, fight-or-flight behavior favors faster responses, which is why you may be defensive and sometimes regret the things that have been said in arguments.

Sleep is also a major factor in stress management. It allows you to restart and wake up with a clearer mind. When your sleep is lacking, attention, self-control, and memory will be negatively affected. When you are well-rested, it is easier to be creative, positive, and proactive when confronting a toxic person.

Focus on Solutions Instead of Not Problems

Did you know that, ultimately, where you focus your attention, determines what emotional state you are going to be in? If you find yourself paying attention to the problems of your life, you create stress and negative emotions for yourself. When you fixate more on the positive, you end up creating perpetual positive emotions and lower levels of stress! As far as toxic people are concerned, try to avoid focusing on how difficult they can be. This only leads to them having power over you. Instead, see if you can regain control by coming up with a mature method of handling them.

Trust your support system.

You may enjoy the feeling of solving your own problems and being independent, but sometimes it just helps to recognize your personal weaknesses. By doing so, you are likely to turn to your family, friends, and colleagues support system to gain a new perspective. There will always be an individual somewhere who wants the best for you and is willing to give you the resources you need to get out of a difficult situation. Do not be ashamed to request for assistance when you need it, as you never know when someone else's insight can lead to a problem being resolved.

CHAPTER SEVEN

TIPS TO DEALING WITH

MANIPULATION

If you think you may be in a relationship with a person who's trying to manipulate you, we suggest you follow the following steps:

1. Be aware of this and be open-minded. Ask yourself, is this individual really trying to override my choice and make me act the way they want me to? Be aware that there may be a variation between exhortation (strong encouragement) and manipulation.

Exhortation is when someone speaks the truth to you that is to your benefit and then lets you make your own decisions. They accept, regard and respect your final decision, even if they do not agree. Manipulation is when a person tells you something that might be true, but ultimately, it is for their benefit. The key here is that they will not let you make your own decisions, and they will not accept or respect your final decision. They are going to keep pressing until you make the decision that they want you to make.

2. Get input from a licensed consultant. This is particularly important if your spouse or relative is the manipulator. A counselor can help you identify the underlying personal issues that you may

need to address, and they will guide you through the best ways to navigate your interactions with the other person. An outside perspective can help you to see things more clearly.

3. Ask yourself: Is this person safe enough (verbally, physically, emotionally) to confront, or is there going to be a negative backlash against me if I do? The best way to approach conflicts between two people is to confront the person one-on-one. If the person is not safe or you are not sure, follow the advice and do not confront them. Things are likely to be thrown back in your face and blamed on you. Here again, the input of a counselor may be important.

4. Set and enforce sound boundaries. Stop playing the script of the manipulator. Boundaries keep you from being disturbed, and they have consequences for the people who are trying to cross them. The more destructive the manipulation, the stronger the boundary must be. You may need to increase the physical or relational distance between the other person and yourself, even to the point where you stop all contact until their unhealthy manipulative behavior stops.

Persuasion and Emotional Manipulation

People can manipulate others with hundreds of tactics. Some of the most common ones include:

1. Using an intense emotional connection to control the behavior of another person. For example, an abusive person might try to manipulate a person by moving very quickly into a romantic

relationship. They may attract their victim with loving gestures in order to lower their guard or make them feel indebted.

2. Playing on the insecurities of a person. This is a popular technique among advertisers, like when a cosmetic company makes a person feel unattractive or old. It also works well in interpersonal relationships. For example, someone might make their romantic partner think that no one else could ever love them.

3. Lying and denying. Manipulators can bombard their victims with lies. When they are caught, they may deny the lie or cover it up with another falsehood.

4. Hyperbole and generalization. It is hard to respond to the allegation of never "being loving or never working hard. Specific details can be discussed, while vague accusations are often more difficult to dispute.

5. To change the subject. In an argument about one's behavior, an individual may turn his attention to attacking his critic. The deflection often takes the form, "Well, what about [X]?" For example, if a spouse expresses concern about their partner's use of drugs, the partner may attack the parenting skills of their spouse.

6. Move the goalposts. This happens when a manipulative individual constantly shifts the criteria that must be met in order to satisfy them. For example, a tyrant may use his coworker's clothes as an excuse to harass them. If an individual changes his or her outfits, he

may claim that the person will not deserve "professional respect until he changes his hairstyle, accent, or another miscellaneous trait.

7. Use fear to control someone else. For example, a person may use threats of violence or physically intimidating body language.

8. Use social inequities to control another person. For example, a neurotypical person may attempt to use cognitive disability to demean or dismiss another person's experience.

9. Passive aggression. This is a broad aspect of behavior that includes a number of strategies, such as guilt-tripping, giving backhanded compliments. Passive-aggression is a way of expressing displeasure or anger without directly expressing emotion.

10. Giving someone the silent treatment. It is all right to ask for time to think about an argument or tell someone who has deeply hurt you that you do not want to talk to them anymore. Ignoring someone to punish them or make them fearful is a manipulative tactic.

11. Gaslights. Gaslighting involves causing the victim to doubt their own understanding of reality. For example, an abusive person might deny that the abuse has occurred, telling the victim that something is wrong with their memory.

12. Recruiting other people to help with manipulation. For example, an abusive parent might ask family members to remind the child how much the parent sacrificed for the child. Social pressure may convince the child to stop complaining about abusive behavior.

Such tactics may be combined or alternated by a manipulative person depending on the context.

The Dark End

The Dark of the Moon is considered a particularly mysterious, fruitful and flexible time to mold the creative experiences that will come in the weeks immediately ahead. It is said that wishes made to the last sliver of the Moon's light fade to the left, and affirmed through the Dark of the Moon period, until the first sliver of new light appears again to the right, have special support — special empowerment — to come true. Affirming them again at the time of the New Moon itself gives extra impetus to their nourishment and initiative.

The Dark of the Moon is a time of legendary power for this kind of creation. The Dark of the Moon is always best suited to rest, to recover, to be quiet, to invite calm and serenity to your world, and to spend some time in personal reflection looking back on your life and your personal history — as far as you want to go into the past — and to play with new intentions, new desires, new directions. It is time to stay at home—physically and psychologically — and tend to your private world and its circumstances.

Create conditions that will fill your mind, and indulge them fully, whether it means meditation, reading, contemplation, cleansing, clearing away the emotional and psychological debris that hinders you, listening to music, writing in your personal journal, talking quietly to intimate, trusted associates, listening to the whispered words of your deepest intuitions, working on personal healing therapies and rituals, or a combination of all these things.

Play with ideas and think about things that you might want to create over the next few weeks and realize that this is a time for brainstorming, daydreaming, and fantasizing, not a time for taking action. All the stuff begins in the mind. Everything in the world originated from the nebulous intellectual energy of an idea, a dream, a desire.

CONCLUSION

People are trying to get you to do things through persuasion and manipulation, and you may not even be aware of it if you are adept. You have to teach people how to treat you. If you accept a certain behavior, then you give an indication that it is acceptable to you. You ha ve got to figure out who these people are and why they are doing what they are doing. Look for signs when you are persuaded to do something you would not normally do. Are you giving out signs that what they are doing is all right because you are tolerating their behavior? Your response to people is what gives them the knowledge of what you will or will not allow them to do.

Now that you know the manipulative people in your life, how do you deal with them? Dealing with manipulative people can be tricky, as it might be someone you really care about, and you do not want to get them out of your life. When someone gets you to do something that you do not want to do, you need to tell him what he is doing. Patterns develop in your interactions with people who are hard to break, but you will need to be determined to change the way you react and what you allow people to do. Be clear to the person that your behavior is going to change regardless of whether it changes. You can only take control of your own actions. You cannot change someone else. They are only going to change if they want to change, but you do not have to keep on acting in a way that makes you uncomfortable.

If you have confronted the person and they have not changed the way they are acting with you. You have to decide what you can tolerate, and this depends very much on your relationship with the person. If they are a big part of your life versus a casual acquaintance, you are going to react differently. If they are not critical in your life, you might just want to distance yourself from them. If they are a family member or your spouse, it is harder, if not impossible, to get them out of your life. You still have control over whether you allow yourself to continue to be manipulated. You just need to stop responding in the way they expect when they are trying to manipulate you. The response you might get when you stop reacting as they expect you to do, is they might try to make you believe you are the one with the problem, not them. To be true to yourself, you must stand firm and trust your instincts. I hope now that you will be able to understand the tricks and techniques used to identify this set of people and how you can escape from their clutches.

Made in the USA
Coppell, TX
01 February 2021